CEDRIC'S CIRCUS A E

CW00383811

Written by JIM WYLLIE
Illustrated by MIGGIE WYLLIE

SEAFARER BOOKS

© Jim and Miggie Wyllie 2008

Published in the UK by Seafarer Books Ltd
102 Redwald Road, Rendlesham, Suffolk IP12 2TE

www.seafarerbooks.com

ISBN 978-1-906266-07-3

A CIP record for this book is available from the British Library

By the same authors:
Cedric the Seahorse
Cedric's Day at the Castle
Cedric's Adventure at Sea

Editing, Hugh Brazier
Typesetting and design, Simon Robertson-Young
Printed in China by Asia Graphic Printing Ltd

'Grandpa,' said Polly to me one day,
'Can we ask Cedric the Seahorse to play?
There's a circus in town and it would be fun,
to give a big treat to all of our chums.'

1

Polly went off to to send Cedric the sign,
the one you all know, made from clothes on the line.
Then to our secret place, just round the bend,
to meet Cedric and Glad and all of our friends.

And there on the beach were Cedric and Glad,
with our friendly dragon called Dan Heselblad
and Pedro the puppy, who's nearly a dog,
with Peter the Penguin and Willy the frog.

3

Jemima hopped up and wanted to know,
what was the plan and please could she go?
'We are going,' I said, 'to a circus in town,
to see wonderful acts and a funny old clown!'

Cedric said, 'Gosh! what a splendid idea
but let's try some tricks of our own over here.
I'll show you some things that I did as a lad –
so he took off his coat and gave it to Glad.

5

Cedric tried tumbling and walked on his hands,
his tail in the air and his head near the sand.
A seagull came by and perched on his toes
but Cedric collapsed when a crab bit his nose!

He rolled on the ground and we all laughed with glee
as the seagull flew off to his friends out at sea.
Glad had a go, juggling shells that she found,
while we watched with awe, not making a sound.

Jemima was thrilled and joined in the fun,
then Dan tried a trick rolling smoke off his tongue.
It curled in the air, formed a ring of such size,
that he flew through the middle, to our great surprise!

8

Peter and Pedro then made up a game,
of make-believe horses with green seaweed manes.
Willy the frog jumped high on their backs
and rode round and round like a real circus act.

9

We set off for town and there on the green
was the circus big top, the largest we'd seen.
With side shows and dodgems and things all around
and a man wearing stilts, ten feet off the ground!

Cedric and Glad came with Polly and me,
to drive in the dodgems as fast as could be.
She spun the car round and to make matters worse,
roared off again – this time in reverse!

Polly and Cedric decided to try
and win a big prize at the coconut shy.
Cedric threw balls both to left and to right,
giving a man the most terrible fright!

We then took our seats at the edge of the ring
and the circus began when the horses came in.
There were chestnuts and greys that trotted in pairs,
blue plumes on their backs and red by their ears!

Next came the clowns with their broken-down car,
that collapsed in the ring puffing smoke in the air.
They wore battered old hats and baggy checked suits
and had on their feet the most e–nor–mous boots.

14

The ringmaster said, 'I am pleased to announce
a world famous act is about to commence.
So please will you welcome Miss Lily van Tropp,
who will walk the high wire, in our circus big top.'

We all clapped our hands and Miss Lily bowed low,
her costume of gold in the lights seemed to glow.
She climbed very fast, right into the sky
to where the wire gleamed – it was ever so high.

The audience hushed as she stepped into space.
Way up on the wire she moved with such grace.
But half-way across, she faltered and stopped –
something was wrong in the circus big top.

Miss Lily was stuck, she was held fast like glue
and nobody seemed to know what to do.
Then Cedric announced, 'I have a plan.'
And the audience gasped as he climbed onto Dan.

'I'll fly to Miss Lily, upon Dan's broad back,
and bring her down here, it's as simple as that.'
The audience hushed as Dan spread his wings
for a dragon in flight is a very rare thing.

19

They rescued Miss Lily as Cedric had planned,
and the audience cheered as they came in to land.
She burst into tears, then kissed Cedric's cheek –
he turned bright red and rushed back to his seat!

20

We joined the parade and marched round the ring,
then everyone clapped and started to sing,
of Cedric and Dan, who were ever so brave
and Lily von Tropp who they'd managed to save.

21

And as we walked home it started to snow –
great flakes of white, that gradually grew
and covered the ground, until it was white,
making the town a magical sight.
But now as we reach our story's end,
it's **good-night to Polly and all of her friends.**